The Little Flower Bulb

Helping Children Bereaved by Suicide

Eleanor Gormally
Visuals by Loki & Splink

VERITAS

Published 2011 by
Veritas Publications
7–8 Lower Abbey Street
Dublin 1
Ireland

publications@veritas.ie
www.veritas.ie

ISBN 978-1-84730-260-1

10 9 8 7 6 5 4 3 2 1

A catalogue record for this book is available from the British
Library.

Designed by Lir Mac Cárthaigh, Veritas
Printed in Ireland by Walsh Colour Print, Co. Kerry

Veritas books are printed on paper made from the wood pulp of managed
forests. For every tree felled, at least one tree is planted, thereby renewing
natural resources.

Jamie pushes his favourite bear into the outer pouch of his rucksack.

'Off we go, Ted,' he whispers quietly, 'just you and me now.'

Jamie looks at his clock. It's very early in the morning. The big hand points to ten. The little hand points to five.

He checks the day on his calendar. Friday.

He pulls back the curtain to see if all is clear.

Then he checks his supplies.

* 1 red **apple**
* 1 bag of sticky **toffees**
* 1 bottle of fizzy **water**
* 1 **torch** – *pocket size*
* 2 **chocolate bars**
* 1 warm **jumper**
* 1 **sleeping bag**
* **wellie boots** (*get from garden shed*)

Gone to My treehouse

Jamie

As he pins the note to his pillow, Jamie thinks about why he is going to the treehouse ...

✗ **Mum** *is too busy*

✗ **Twins** *are too* **NOISY**

✗ School *is* BORING

✗ Friends are stupid

✗ He misses his Dad ...

'Goodbye room,' he sighs, closing his bedroom door gently.

'**Got to get my boots**,' Jamie tells Ted as they leave the quiet house.

The light from his torch hops and bounces in the dark.

Following the grey stone path, Jamie heads straight for the garden shed.

Once inside, he spots Dad's things ...

Jamie laughs as he prances around in **Dad's big garden boots**.

He itches his head as he tugs **Dad's woolly cap** over his ears.

He grins as he wriggles his fingers into **Dad's gloves**, and makes monster faces at Ted.

Suddenly Jamie stops. '**I wish …**' he mutters to himself. '**I wish Dad …**' he says, '**I wish Dad was HERE!**' He kicks one of Dad's flowerpots really hard. The pot flies high into the air and lands with a loud **tHumP!**

Jamie panics. Bits of pottery fall everywhere. Some bits fall on the garden chair ...

Other bits land on the lawnmower. Some bits drop onto Dad's toolbox.

Grabbing Ted, Jamie scurries under the workbench. '**What will Dad say?**' he thinks. Then he remembers. Dad is dead. Jamie feels terrible.

Just then, out of the corner of his eye, Jamie notices one of Dad's flower bulbs **rolling** across the timber floor. He reaches out for it, but stops. He hears someone coming.

'Jaaamie?'
'Jamie, where *are* you?' Sofie calls out.

Seeing the light in the garden shed, Sofie rushes in and finds Jamie. '**What's that?**' she asks, spotting the bulb. '**Don't touch it!**' yells Jamie. He grabs the small bulb and stuffs it in his pocket. '**That's mine! I saw it first!**'

Carrying a sleepy Meg, Mum follows closely behind Sofie.

'**I found your note**,' she says to Jamie, stroking his spiky hair. Then Meg wakes. She sees Jamie's rucksack. '**I'm hungry**,' she whinges. '**Oh Meg, my pet**,' sighs Mum wearily, '**I don't have anything for you to eat!**'

Jamie looks from Mum to Sofie to Meg. He opens his rucksack and carefully unwraps his packed food. He sits up on the wooden bench and makes space for the others. Mum tucks the sleeping bag around their knees as they all squash close together.

One by one, Jamie, Sofie, Meg and Mum **bite** into the **juicy apple**.
One by one, they **chew** the **sticky toffees**.
One by one, they **munch** the **chocolate**.

'**I'm sorry, Mum**,' Jamie says. '**I broke Dad's pot. And I think the lawnmower is scratched, and**,' he admits guiltily, '**Dad's shed is a mess!**' Mum looks around at all Dad's things. Then she looks back at Jamie. '**It's all right**,' she says, giving him a little nudge, '**we can clean it up … just you and me!**'

Jamie snuggles into Mum.

'**I miss Dad!**' he whispers.

'**I know**,' Mum says, '**I miss him too**.'

'**Mum**,' Jamie asks in a low voice, '**why did Dad ...**' he pauses, '**you know**.'

'**Take his own life?**' Mum asks softly. Jamie nods.

'**Dad's mind was ill**,' Mum answers. '**He wasn't himself**.' She stops for a minute. '**Did you know**,' she says, '**that all our thoughts and feelings come from our brain?**' Jamie shakes his head in amazement.

'**Well they do**,' explains Mum, '**but Dad's brain got very sick. And his feelings got all jumbled up. He wasn't able to think very clearly. And he didn't know how to talk about how bad he felt**.'

'**But he never said goodbye to me**.' Jamie wipes his nose on his sleeve. '**And now**,' he says, '**he'll never get to see my play. I hate him!**'

'**You know**,' Mum says thoughtfully, '**Dad was very proud of you. He loved us all to bits. But his illness stopped him from feeling our love**.'

'**Mum?**' Jamie frowns, '**will you go too?**'

'**No, Jamie**,' Mum answers gently, '**I'm here for keeps**.'

'**Jamie's crying!**' Meg interrupts, pointing her chubby little finger at her big brother's tears. '**Why's he crying?**'

'**Jamie's sad**,' Mum says, taking Meg's hand, '**because Dad has died and we won't see him again**.'

'**I cried when I cut my knee!**' Meg yells, lifting her leg. Then she catches the edge of the plaster and pulls it off. '**Look! It's all better now**.'
'**And I cried when I lost Dolly!**' Sofie chips in, hugging her rag doll.

It is getting late.
Everyone is quiet.
Jamie remembers his bulb.
He takes it out of his pocket
and turns it around in his
hand.

'**What sort of flower bulb
do you think it is?**' he asks.
'**I wonder!**' says Mum.
'**I know**,' Jamie declares
excitedly, '**let's plant it
and see!**'

And so, as the silver stars shine in the dark sky, Mum watches while Jamie and the twins **plant the bulb**.

Autumn turns to winter and the little family watch the ground where their bulb has been planted and wait for spring.

As the shoots push up through the dark soil, **they wait**. As the small green leaves appear, **they wait**.

As the buds begin to open, **they imagine** what the flower might be.

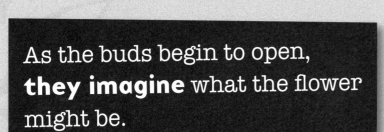

Then one morning in March, it happens! The little bulb has become **a beautiful flower**.

'**Dad's favourite!**' beams Jamie.
'**I know**,' replies Mum.

Mum and Jamie realise immediately what they have to do. So that evening the little family make a very special journey.

Together they place the flower on Dad's grave. Their golden daffodil blows gently in the breeze. **They remember Dad and smile**.